THE INDUSTRIAL REVOLUTION, MIGRATION, AND IMMIGRATION

Nick Christopher

PowerKiDS
press™

NEW YORK

Published in 2016 by The Rosen Publishing Group, Inc.
29 East 21st Street, New York, NY 10010

Editor: Katie Kawa
Book Design: Katelyn E. Reynolds

Photo Credits: Cover, pp. 9, 10, 13 (top), 15, 17, 19 courtesy of the Library of Congress; p. 5 MPI/Getty Images;
p. 6 Hulton Archive/Getty Images; p. 7 ArtMechanic/Wikimedia Commons; p. 11 SuperStock/Getty Images;
p. 13 (bottom) FPG/Hulton Archive/Getty Images; p. 16 Shirtwaist/Wikimedia Commons; p. 21 Victoria Lipov/
Shutterstock.com; p. 22 Everett Historical/Shutterstock.com.

Cataloging-in-Publication Data

Christopher, Nick.
The Industrial revolution, migration, and immigration / by Nick Christopher.
p. cm. — (Spotlight on immigration and migration)
Includes index.
ISBN 978-1-5081-4086-3 (pbk.)
ISBN 978-1-5081-4087-0 (6-pack)
ISBN 978-1-5081-4088-7 (library binding)
1. Industrial revolution — United States — Juvenile literature. 2. Foreign workers — United States — History
— Juvenile literature. 3. United States — Emigration and immigration — History — Juvenile literature. I.
Christopher, Nick. II. Title.
HC105.C45 2016
330.973'05—d23

Manufactured in the United States of America

CPSIA Compliance Information: Batch #BW16PK: For further information contact Rosen Publishing, New York, New York at 1-800-237-9932.

CONTENTS

FROM FARMS TO FACTORIES

When early settlers first began to **immigrate** to the United States, they were met with open land that they soon turned into farms. For many years, the U.S. economy depended on agriculture, or farming. Life in America was centered on farms. This meant that frosts, floods, or other natural causes could destroy crops and harm the economy.

In the 1800s, the Industrial Revolution, which had begun in Great Britain in the mid-1700s, began to take hold in America. The discovery of new power sources, such as steam power and electricity, made the production of goods faster and more efficient. As the Industrial Revolution spread throughout the United States, people began to migrate from farms to cities, which became the centers of American industry.

Factories such as the one shown here were common sights in American cities during the Industrial Revolution. People migrated from farms and **emigrated** from other countries to find work in American factories during this time.

5

ACROSS THE ATLANTIC

Britain was the birthplace of the Industrial Revolution. Inventions that came from Britain, such as James Hargreaves's **spinning jenny** and James Watt's improved steam engine, forever changed the way goods were produced.

Improvements to the spinning jenny, shown here, allowed people to go from spinning eight threads at once to spinning 80 threads at once!

While industries were growing in Britain and across Europe, life wasn't improving for everyone who lived there. In fact, the Industrial Revolution in Europe made cities overcrowded, which made living conditions unhealthy. Many people left Europe to find work in America once the Industrial Revolution spread across the Atlantic Ocean. From 1840 to 1860, around 4 million immigrants came to America from European countries such as Britain, Ireland, and Germany. They hoped to find a better life in the United States.

This 19th-century painting shows the smoke rising from factories in Britain during the Industrial Revolution.

CHANGES IN COTTON

After the Industrial Revolution began in Britain, it didn't take long for it to spread to the United States. By the end of the 1700s, Americans were beginning to grow more and more excited by what machines could do. Both immigrants and those who were born in the United States contributed to the growth of American industry.

Samuel Slater was a British immigrant. He built the first water-powered **textile** mill in 1790 in Pawtucket, Rhode Island. Slater's mill used machines to spin cotton into thread, and it's known as the first real U.S. factory. In 1793, a New Englander named Eli Whitney invented the cotton gin, which cleaned cotton by removing its seeds. These men and their inventions helped the factory system grow in the United States.

Whitney's cotton gin helped cotton grow into a very important crop in the South. This led to an increase in the number of slaves needed to pick the cotton and use the gin, which is short for "engine."

MIGRATING TO CITIES

Cities began to grow as the Industrial Revolution took hold in the United States. People started to migrate from **rural** parts of America to find work in the cities.

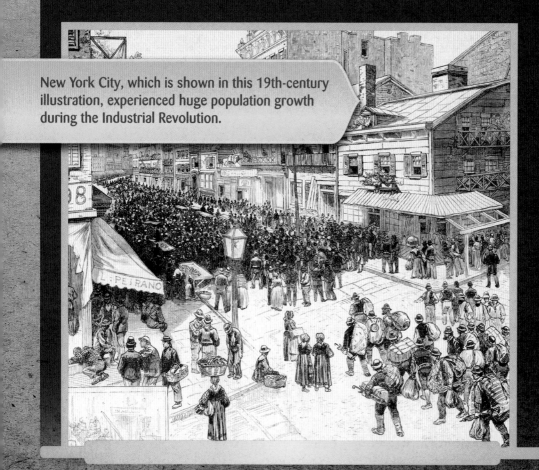

New York City, which is shown in this 19th-century illustration, experienced huge population growth during the Industrial Revolution.

The invention of farm machinery, such as the tractor, made farming faster and cheaper than before. Many farmworkers were no longer needed. They had to look for work in steel mills, textile factories, and other industries. These industries were often centered in cities, including New York City, Pittsburgh, Boston, and Chicago. Workers didn't need to have many skills to perform most factory jobs. This allowed the former farmworkers who migrated to cities to find work in factories—even though they had no experience with the machines in them.

Pittsburgh became known as the "Steel City" because of the steel mills that were built there during the Industrial Revolution.

LIFE AFTER SLAVERY

During the Industrial Revolution, northern U.S. cities became places of opportunity for African Americans who'd once been slaves. Many people of African **descent** who'd been slaves in the South migrated to the North after they were officially freed in 1865.

Some left the South to escape sharecropping, because they usually ended up in **debt** to their former masters. A sharecropper is someone who farms other people's land. They're given credit for things such as tools and seeds. At harvest, they receive part of the value of the crop as pay. Some of these earnings are then used to repay the credit. Other former slaves left the South because they were the targets of attacks. They hoped to find a better life working in northern factories.

Many African Americans migrated to northern cities because they felt working in factories would be better than working as sharecroppers.

ON THE MOVE

Some inventions that came out of the Industrial Revolution made the production of goods easier. Others improved transportation and communication. These inventions made immigration and migration easier.

The steam **locomotive** was invented in 1804. Throughout the 1800s, the laying of several railroad systems across the United States helped people migrate throughout the country for work. People were able to move from job to job. Also, the invention of the steamship made it quicker and easier for people to emigrate from other countries.

The inventions of the telephone, **telegraph**, and improved printing methods helped spread the word about job openings and opportunities in new factories. During the Industrial Revolution, information and people got from place to place more quickly than ever before.

Railroads allowed Americans to migrate to growing cities in large numbers. They also allowed immigrants to travel from the ports where they reached the United States to many other places in the country.

A HARD LIFE

While the Industrial Revolution created many new jobs in factories, the working conditions in those factories were often poor. Jobs in factories were generally boring and repetitive. People worked for 12 hours or more each day, six days per week. They weren't paid very much for their work.

Factories were often dirty, dark, and unsafe. For example, a fire at New York City's Triangle Shirtwaist Factory in 1911 killed 146 workers. The only exit for those workers was a locked door, so they had no way to get out.

Child labor was also a problem. It wasn't uncommon for children as young as five to work in factories. Most child labor in the United States was finally banned in 1938 with the passage of the Fair Labor Standards Act.

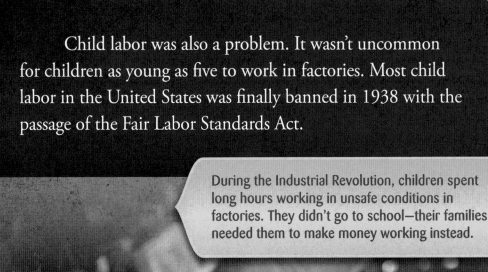

During the Industrial Revolution, children spent long hours working in unsafe conditions in factories. They didn't go to school—their families needed them to make money working instead.

COMING TO AMERICA

Immigrants came to the United States during the Industrial Revolution because they saw it as a land of new opportunities. They were often trying to escape a hard life in Europe or other parts of the world. However, the life many found in the United States was also hard. Many immigrants had little money. They often lived in crowded, dirty buildings called tenements.

Before 1880, most immigrants came from western and northern European countries such as Germany, Ireland, Britain, and Sweden. After 1880, as travel and communication grew easier, immigrants came from southern and eastern European countries such as Italy, Poland, and Greece. These immigrants often found jobs in the factories of America's biggest cities, and they began to build a life for themselves in their new country.

From 1866 to 1915, about 25 million immigrants came to America. They often lived in large cities such as New York City, shown here around 1900.

19

STICKING TOGETHER

Life wasn't easy for immigrants in the United States during the Industrial Revolution. They had to deal with **persecution**, low wages, and sometimes violent treatment before they were accepted by American society.

Many immigrants tried to keep the **traditions** of their homeland. They celebrated traditional holidays, read newspapers in their native language, and ate **ethnic** food. They often settled in communities with others from their country. These neighborhoods had names such as Little Italy or Little Poland, after the places from which the immigrants came. Although many immigrants tried to learn English to help them at their job, they still spoke their native language at home. Sticking together in this new country helped immigrants feel less alone and more connected to their **cultural** roots.

New York City's Little Italy neighborhood was a place where Italian immigrants could preserve their traditional culture in the United States. It's still known for its Italian roots.

AN INDUSTRIAL POWER

When the Industrial Revolution reached the United States, the people of this country were ready to embrace the changes that came with it. Americans were open to new ideas and new ways of doing things. This gave the United States a huge advantage in the Industrial Revolution.

The Industrial Revolution changed the United States forever. By 1900, the United States had become a leading industrial power. More people were migrating to American cities than ever before. Immigrants were arriving in large numbers. New inventions were making life easier for people across the United States. The Industrial Revolution was one of the most important times in American history, and this period helped America grow into the powerful country it still is today.

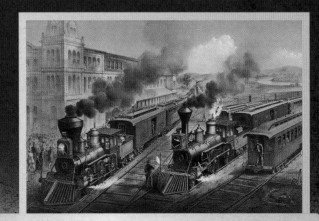

GLOSSARY

cultural: Having to do with the beliefs and ways of life of a group of people.

debt: The state of owing money.

descent: The background of a person in terms of their family or nationality.

emigrate: To leave a country or region to live somewhere else.

ethnic: Belonging to a certain group of people who have a culture that is different from the main culture of a country.

immigrate: To come to a country to live there.

locomotive: The vehicle that produces the power that pulls a train.

persecution: The act of being treated cruelly or unfairly, especially because of race, culture, or beliefs.

rural: Of or relating to the country.

spinning jenny: A machine that used more than one spindle at a time to spin thread.

telegraph: A system of sending messages over long distances by using wires and electrical signals.

textile: A kind of cloth that is woven or knit.

tradition: A belief or way of doing things that is handed down.

INDEX

PRIMARY SOURCE LIST

Page 7
Coalbrookdale by Night. Created by Philip James de Loutherbourg. 1801. Oil on canvas. Now kept at the Science Museum, London, United Kingdom.

Page 16
The Triangle Shirtwaist Factory Fire. Creator unknown. Original photograph taken on March 25, 1911. First published on the front page of *The New York World* on March 26, 1911.

Page 17
"Carrying-in" boy in Alexandria Glass Factory, Alexandria, Virginia. Created by Lewis Wickes Hine. June 1911. Photograph. Now kept at the Library of Congress Prints and Photographs Division, Washington, D.C.

Page 19
Mulberry Street, New York City. Published by Detroit Publishing Co. ca. 1900. Color print from black-and-white photographic negative. Now kept at the Library of Congress Prints and Photographs Division, Washington, D.C.

WEBSITES

Due to the changing nature of Internet links, PowerKids Press has developed an online list of websites related to the subject of this book. This site is updated regularly. Please use this link to access the list: www.powerkidslinks.com/soim/irmi